Handmade In *The Present Moment*

"When I first met Yvette one of the first things I noticed was her passion for what she was about to embark upon. Passion is key and Yvette is one that radiates it when it comes to being of service and helping others. Her heart was present the moment I met her, and has only gotten bigger with every successful year the café continues to serve the masses. With this warm approach to all she does, her team truly is a family, and have really created that atmosphere with The Present Moment Café.

I am so happy to call Yvette a dear friend, and my hat goes off to her and her team for the incredible work they continue to do by being plant activists, sharing their truth through food, one bite at a time"

-Chad Sarno
Chef, consultant, plant activist

dedicated to my mother Elizabeth (Elishoo), my greatest teacher
September 29, 1913 – July 15, 2004

Acknowledgements

I credit Chad Sarno for laying the foundation of the café. He gave me confidence through his expert training and knowledge to create my living foods restaurant.

To Harold Locke and his crew for reconstructing a warehouse into an eco-friendly dining room.

To Walter O'kon for his enthusiasm as architect of the "raw food bar."

To Richard Lang for his fine craftsmanship of my bamboo bar.

To Lisa Millet for her brilliant painting which transformed a structure into a work of art.

To James Beach who piece by piece cut glass (and his fingers) for shaping the stunning curtains of the stained glass which became our logo.

To Aris LaTham who, in sharing his raw soul, guided me back to the garden.

To Molly Jane Hammond, our graphic designer and chef, whose talented hands are visible all over this book inside and out.

To my friends and editors Susan "Hawkeye" Ross and Patty "Sissor Hands" Hart.

To my creative chefs past and present who have used their hands and hearts to develop the great dishes we continue to serve daily.

To the wonderful staff of dishwashers and servers who take care to welcome our guests as if into their own living rooms.

We wish to thank our beautiful and gracious customers who have supported us, applauded us, believed in us and shared their love of the Present Moment café with their friends and family.

It is truly a pleasure to feed you.

And finally, to my son Nathan who to this day continues to prod me to live in the moment with love and gratitude.....and patience.

contents

past

(10)

present

future

(84)

Foreword

I will state, with utmost sincerity, that I was honored to be asked to write the foreword to this fine book you are holding in your hands: *Handmade in the Present Moment*. My involvement with the birth of the café extends back prior to its opening - to the raw potluck mentioned by Yvette - rife with bagged lettuce and dehydrated hockey pucks. The date was January 14th, 2006, which, looking back, turned out to be a watershed moment in my own personal journey on this path.

Before that date listed above, I had been introduced to raw food via the writings of health crusaders Michael O'Brien, Howard Loomis, and Edward Howell (among others) in March of 2002. "The human race is at least half-sick," wrote Edward Howell in his magnum opus, *Enzyme Nutrition*. "In a biological sense, there are no completely healthy people living on the convetional diet."

These two sentences, coupled with the following 192 pages of Howell's lively academic prose, had enough of my attention when I was a 24-year old college student searching for answers about health and nutrition.

After combing through the medical literature and testing my own diet out with increases in fruits and vegetables, I was left with an uncomfortable feeling that everything I knew about nutrition had been wrong. Twenty-four years of counting calories, worrying about macronutrients, and ensuring I had the proper vitamin/mineral intake (coupled with watching loved ones pass away long before their time from dietary related illness), led me to realize that I had to first "unwind" these false notions of healthy eating for myself (key word) before I could ever go out and spread such good news to others. In a world chock-full of misinformation, telling the truth can be seen as a revolutionary act, at times.

And for the record: Yvette and Nate were the very potent dose of truth serum that myself and many others needed in Northeast Florida back in 2006, a time when vegans were an endangered species in town, and raw-foodists were literally unheard of.

The beauty of the *Present Moment Café* is that during these past five years, it has encompassed a feeling of "inclusiveness" that welcomes omnivores and vegans alike, travelers and homemakers, professionals and students, young and elderly, and everyone in-between. To view those who dine there on any given evening is to view a snapshot of our culture: diverse in their very own nature, and collective in sharing superb food and excellent company. It is genuine fine-dining without the pompous attitude.

In closing, I would like to acknowledge this recipe book as one that has been eagerly anticipated by many for quite some time now. As the café has grown during these past five years, so has our community in their understanding and desire for this kind cuisine.

And, while many fantastic raw recipe books on the market have graced my kitchen and have inspired me greatly, I anxiously await when the magic of the *Present Moment's* food, via this book, will be my number one choice to reach for when I am craving a meal to please my senses. I entrust that you will find the same excitement when delving into the creative pages that lie ahead.

Eternally,
Ian M. Keogh
Academic Dean Fortis College
Raw Foodist, Jacksonville's Raw & Living Foods Group
www.jaxraw.com

Chad Sarno and Yvette Schindler

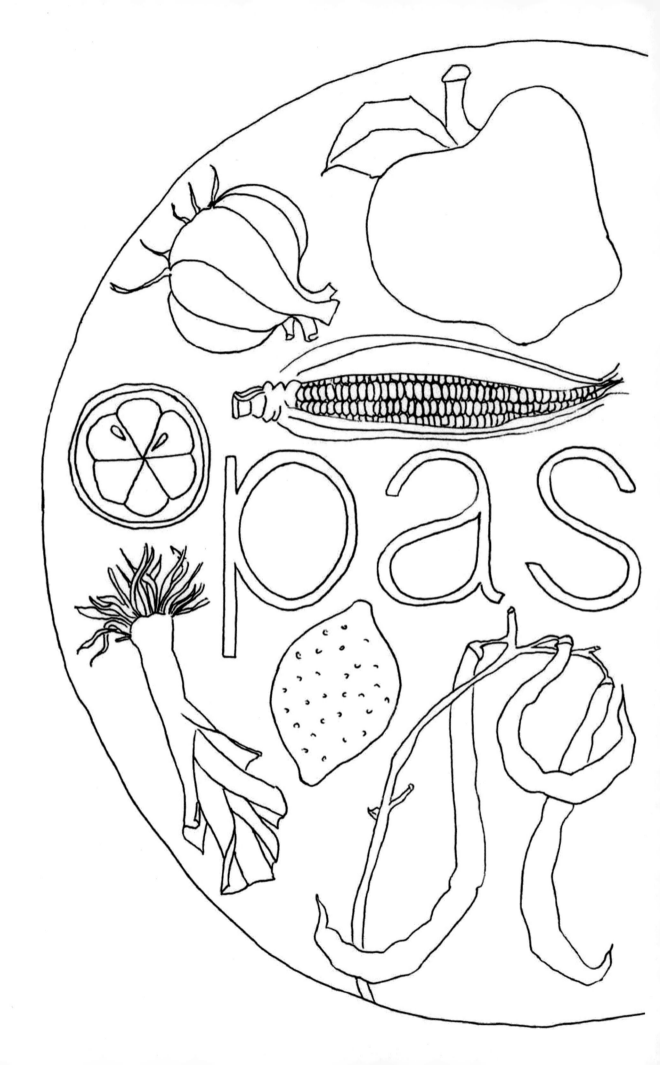

Introduction

Many hands were involved in creating the *Present Moment Café*. Each one touched the others, forming a lineage for which I pay homage and gratitude.

It began with my son Nathan handing me a book,
The cover had three young men in a plush jungle tree.

"Read this Mom," he said, with a rather serious look on his face.
"Okay. I'll get to it."
"No, you have to read it now." He was serious.

The last time he had asked me to read a book he
was 3 years old. Now at eighteen he was a full foot taller than I, and I had to look up at him. I felt like the kid; I sat down and read.

Halfway through the book, I told him I couldn't read any more....it was too radical. Every chapter ended with the words, "Cooked food is poison."

"Please—read it to the end," Nathan insisted, looking down at me.

Having just come out of a divorce with his father of twenty years, I felt it was important to be on the same page so to speak, so I finished the book. I was intrigued with the simplicity of the concept. Raw food, our original food, made perfect sense, but I was skeptical of the glowing reported results.

So we set out to go 100% raw vegan for the three months of summer...in the Deep South BBQ country. We purchased stacks of raw food recipe books, videos, and tapes. From our kitchen cabinets, we hung bags of soaked nuts and sprouts.

We were blending, juicing, sprouting, marinating, fermenting, and dehydrating until our kitchen turned into a science laboratory. Our friends, who were unable to understand our new concept, scattered like bacteria in a Petri dish.

We spent a lot of time alone in our laboratory. When his father stopped by to see how we were doing, his suspicions were verified. I had gone nuts and taken his son with me.

[1] Stephen Arlin, Fouad Dini, David Wolfe, R.C. Dini, Nature's First Law (Maul Brothers Publishing; 6th edition, 2003) 234.

It was at this time that we were also inspired by the movie *What the Bleep Do We Know* and Masaru Emoto's book *Messages From Water*[2], so Nathan and I decided to conduct our own experiment.

We placed two bowls of cherries on our counter. One bowl was given feelings of love and gratitude and the other was rejected and ignored. The loved bowl of cherries stayed fresh three to four days longer than the denounced one. True story. It was the same batch of cherries.

However, this wasn't surprising to me. I recalled that when I was young, I would watch my mother cook, which she did often, as I was the youngest of eight children. For the longest time I thought she was mumbling to herself during the cooking process until I discovered that she was actually praying over the food.

As she stirred the rice, she invoked the grace of God in the Aramaic language. She would make the sign of the cross over the grape leaves we had rolled together as if it were part of the recipe.

My mother's food was delicious. When relatives asked her why their dishes didn't come out tasting like hers, even though they followed her recipe, she would say, "*bee tha*" which meant, "by your hand." She explained that it's the feeling you hold in your hand which affects the final dish. If my mother were alive today, she would see how much of a hand she had in my life. I was a loved bowl of cherries!

Now my other mother had a hand in my life. Mother Nature's diet was changing me. I was feeling younger and more vibrant. For one, I no longer needed an alarm clock. I just woke up when I needed to, and I awoke feeling fresh and alive, unlike Dracula's daughter, squinting puffy-eyed at sunlight.

The most remarkable change I was noticing was the lack of pain from the arthritis in my right knee, which had hurt every time I walked up steps. It was something I thought I surely had to live with since my mother had it. A major benefit was ditching the fifteen pounds that I could never seem to lose on a high protein, low carb diet, or any of the many diets I had tried.

[2] http://www.life-enthusiast.com/twilight/research_emoto.htm

My cellulite was gone...I repeat: cellulite was gone. But what was most pronounced was the skin on my face. Before eating predominantly raw, it was blotched and un-evenly toned; now my skin was soft, even-toned, and hydrated.

I was not the only one noticing the changes. Comments from those who saw me were that my skin was glowing, my eyes were bright, and the white in my eyes was whiter. My mind was clearer than ever. A fog had lifted, and the all male employees who worked for me at my boating supply store were stumped.

How could my high energy come from "rabbit food?" My hair was looking exceptionally lustrous, and all my clothes fit nicely. My arms looked as if I worked out with weights, and I seemed to stand up straighter, but, more importantly, I wasn't afraid. I didn't feel prey to anything. I felt like the queen of the jungle.

Nathan had similar results. He was toned and tanned like Tarzan. His blemishes had cleared up. His brown eyes were vibrant like those of a soulful animal living in the present moment. He started photographing halos, which he saw around flowers and trees and objects in nature, that I didn't see. He didn't speak very much and when he did, it was usually on the merits of raw chocolate coming to us at a time when we needed it most to see clearly and to open our hearts. He stated that, "It was truly food of the Gods."

One very clear day as we walked barefoot on the beach, I had an epiphany. Small silvery fish gliding through the shallows reflected the sunlight into my eyes. The squawk of seagulls merged with the sound of children's laughter.

As my feet simultaneously touched water, sand, and sun, I felt grounded to the earth and every living thing. In that moment, I felt a magnetic energy, like electricity running through me. I felt alive in the present moment. I looked up at Nathan and saw the halos he'd been photographing around his head, and I knew that we were experiencing the same feelings, despite our age and gender differences. It was as if we had eaten the same magic mushrooms.

The common denominator was the raw food.

Now what are we going to do? With this new insight, we were at a turning point. Aside from the prestigious *Hippocrates Health Institute* in West Palm Beach, there was no one around the Floridian peninsula who was knowledgeable about raw food, so I started a raw food meet-up group. We had our first potluck with five members. One brought a bag of romaine lettuce hearts straight from the produce section of Winn Dixie. Another brought what appeared to be hockey pucks; dehydrated nuts and vegetables of sorts, which nearly cracked our teeth. Nathan made a "holy" raw chocolate pie, and I served a raw marinara sauce over zucchini noodles with pine nut parmesan (a very common dish in today's raw food circles, but gourmet then). The guests were giddy over the meal.

"Open a restaurant," they cried. "Save us!"

This meet-up group exists today with over five hundred members who are still giddy over their meals at the café.

We were hungry to experience raw food restaurants. Through our investigations, we found that the best place to go was California, that vast shoreline where all new ideas land...off we went.

Rawvolution in Santa Monica was our first stop and a wise choice it was. Matt and Janabai Amsden, having experienced similar results, had created a wonderful restaurant with delicious raw dishes. We ate at over forty raw food restaurants from San Diego to San Francisco, and experienced a vast variety of creative dishes brought forth by people who were touched by the raw food experience.

Finally, we found ourselves at *Café Gratitude*, our last stop. As we were gratefully eating our "I am Thankful" soup with an "I am Fulfilled" salad, we simultaneously saw the writing on the wall. Literally, the words "the present moment" were painted on the wall. "That's it," Nathan said. We had been inspired. We would open a raw food restaurant in our home town of St. Augustine, Florida, the nation's oldest city, with its Fountain of Youth, in one of the most southern states.

"It will be called the Present Moment Café."

Next, I needed to find an educated person who had been eating raw food for a long time. Enter Aris Latham, raw food master chef and a living food vegan for the past 28 years. I was off to the *Sunfire Culinary Institute* in Ocho Rios, Jamaica, for a week intensive with this master. Aris met me at the airport, and as we drove through the lush tropics of Jamaica, he gave me a guided tour of paradise, filled with mangoes, papaya, coconuts, passion fruit, guavas, and jack fruit.

Aris, in his soulful voice, narrated, "The food is cooked already by the sun. When it is ripe, it is ready." He continued, "When you eat God's food in its natural live state, you become fresh and alive yourself. You will regenerate; you will become younger."

Aris was in his sixties and had the body of a much younger man. I had come to the right place to see what I was feeling. The Garden of Eden was alive and well. All the food we need grows naturally for our health and happiness. There was even a forbidden fruit, ackee, which, if eaten before it is ripe, is poisonous. When it naturally cracks open, the fruit is delicious. How wild was all of this!
Aris arranged for me to stay in an old villa on a hilltop overlooking fruit trees and lush grounds. He locked me in at night where I was all alone. There were bars on all the windows and doors. I felt like a caged bird in paradise. He had a library full of new and vintage books on food, philosophy, and nutrition.

For seven days and seven nights, I worked in the garden. Aris arrived in the morning, and we spent eight hours each day soaking, sprouting, marinating, and preparing his famous "Paradise Pies." At night, I read.

I returned from Jamaica with a more developed understanding of my mission. Through the time spent in that garden, I came to realize that my mission stems from my roots. I was born where the Tigris and Euphrates Rivers meet in the area known as the cradle of civilization, purported to be the Garden of Eden.

My grandfather, a Chaldean priest, named me Yvette which means "Little Eve." Little Eve was going to lead us back to the Garden. The best way to get there was to eat our way back home. How I love to eat, but, even more, how I love to feed.

16

The Building

Next to my boating supply store was a storage warehouse. It was to become my "living foods temple." My contractor, Harold Locke, of Native American Salish Tribe descent, and his crew from *Red Bear Construction* gutted the building.

During the process we came upon the first permit for the building issued in 1950, the year of my birth. It was first opened as *The Friendly Bar*. However, it was not so "friendly," as dark skinned people were not allowed service in those days. We also salvaged a panel of jazzy wallpaper from that era, which, along with the permit, hangs in the café. Today, it is truly a "friendly" bar at the *Present Moment Cafe*.

Lisa Millet, a dear friend and extraordinary artist, who knew my Assyrian heritage, painted the walls to reflect a Babylonian temple, which glowed from within. Another friend and artist, James Beach, designed stained glass panels, which we hung in the windows, resembling the Hanging Gardens of Babylon. He crafted a churchlike effect in the cafe, an aesthetic reflection of his Christian devotion.

The Inspectors

Before I could go any further, I had to attend a meeting with the planning and zoning department to receive a permit to turn my warehouse into a café. The meeting was in a small room at City Hall with a big table encircled by large men.

"What kind of restaurant do you want to open?"

I knew this was not going to be easy to explain, and I was told that the less I said, the better off I would be.

"A raw food restaurant."

They were thinking and glancing at each other. A long silence followed. Finally, one of them nodded his head.

"You mean an oyster bar."

"No sir. I mean raw food. There's no cooking, no stoves, no ovens, no frying."

This had never come before them in their entire history of zoning and planning, but they were intent on figuring it out.

"You gonna serve raw meat?"

"No sir. There will be no meat, fish, nor dairy."

They all looked at each other totally perplexed and a bit frustrated.

"Well then whaddya gonna serve?"

"Vegetables, fruits, nuts, seeds." I sighed, remembering the vast fruits and vegetables that even I didn't know existed before Jamaica.

"You want to open a produce stand?"

My wonderful contractor, Harold, leaned in to help me. He cleared his throat and with his calm voice said, "She's thinking of a small café with vegetarian sandwiches, soups, and salads."

This, they could sink their teeth into. They started to come around and eased back in their chairs.

"So like a *Subway* with mostly carry out?"

"No. A real restaurant with seating. I will have a juice bar, which will also serve organic beer and wine." I had thrown another curve ball.

"What is organic beer and wine?" one asked.

"Is there alcohol in it?" asked another.

"It's beer and wine....grown without pesticides. It has alcohol in it."

Little did they know, I was in the midst of a déjà vu...pre-Russian Afghanistan, 1973. I was remembering an intense conversation with a mullah in Kabul as he was questioning my religion. I was a cook in the hotel restaurant that he owned, and had just served him a platter of rice pilaf that I had made. He wanted to know why I was not Muslim, since I had been born in Baghdad. Why was I raised a Christian and also believed in Buddhism and Hinduism? How could I possibly have all of these gods when his belief stated, "There is only one God, and one God only, and that God is Allah."

I was respectful. I did not say, "How can you have so many wives when there is only one husband?" I did say, "In my travels, Imam, I found what you say is true. I believe there is one God..... but many ways to worship Him."

He fingered his worry beads. "Nonsense! These other religions with their monkey gods, mother of God, statues of God ...how ridiculous!"

The other men in the room nodded their heads in agreement even though they didn't understand English. He was an educated and powerful man. If he wanted me to stay or leave that would be the law. "I would explain it as a grain of rice. You can have pilaf, stir fry or steamed rice. It's a cultural way of treating the same grain." He scooped up the rice pilaf between his fingertips and ate it. Thanks be to God that he liked my food! He brushed his hands of the matter, and the conversation ended.

Thirty-two years later I was before the mullahs of my town who believed that there is one food and one food only, and that is cooked. Now I would explain yet another way of eating the grain of rice. You can sprout it! "The food I am going to serve in my restaurant will have already been cooked by the sun. When ripe, it is ready to eat. You don't have to cook it."

They fingered their pencils like worry beads. "If you take a raw almond and place it in the earth, it can sprout. If you heat it beyond 115 degrees, it cannot. It is that life force, or enzymes, or whatever one chooses to call it, that we maintain in the food we serve." I had a very curious audience. "You can feel that energy, and I hope that someday you will give it a try. It's as tasty as cooked food, but it gives you back more." Permission granted.

I was free to open my raw food, sun cooked, living foods restaurant.

Chad Sarno

At this point I didn't want to make any mistakes. Although I had been a macrobiotic chef in Santa Fe and worked in many kitchens in my life, I had never worked in a raw food one. Also, I had tasted some raw food, which, had it been my first introduction, I may never have tried it again. I didn't want that to happen to my customers. Also, I didn't simply want to dangle a raw carrot in front of them and say, "Eat it, it's good for you."

I wanted to bring gourmet raw food to the table, and one name that kept coming up in my research was Chad Sarno. I found him through his recipes. I had tried many different recipes, but his were always the best. He was a graduate of *Living Light Culinary Arts Institute* and continued on as staff chef. Chad was one of the instrumental figures in the recipe development for Roxanne's Restaurant. He was also head chef of Gabriel Cousens' *Tree of Life Café* where he helped develop the culinary arts and apprenticeship program. Chad now works with Whole Foods Market as lead educator with the companies Health Education Program. Chad travels extensively, training chefs and consulting with restaurants around the world. His gourmet cuisine is truly a reflection of the love he puts into everything he prepares. He was the man for the job, and became my new best friend.

Aris fueled the fire in me to go forward with my mission, and Chad gave me the tools, skills and confidence to make it happen. He designed my floor plan. He trained my staff and me on the importance of layering flavors and plating to please the eye. He took the edge off of raw food and made it more mainstream. We customized recipes to suit my preferences and our region. He was a necessary investment.

The Present Moment

In the fall of 2006 we opened the first raw food restaurant in Northeast Florida.
Today there are at least a dozen. We welcome and attract omnivores, vegans, vegetarians
and lovers of fine cuisine. These are the recipes that our café makes daily.
Some are from our kitchen and some are from Chad Sarno's hands on training.
We pass them from our table to yours. All you have to add is *bee tha,* your hand.

In our living room we like to serve all your senses, from the art on the walls to the
tastes and textures on your plate. It is a kitchen with a mission. We love to eat, we love
to feed, and we want to get back to the garden from which we all came.

Yvette

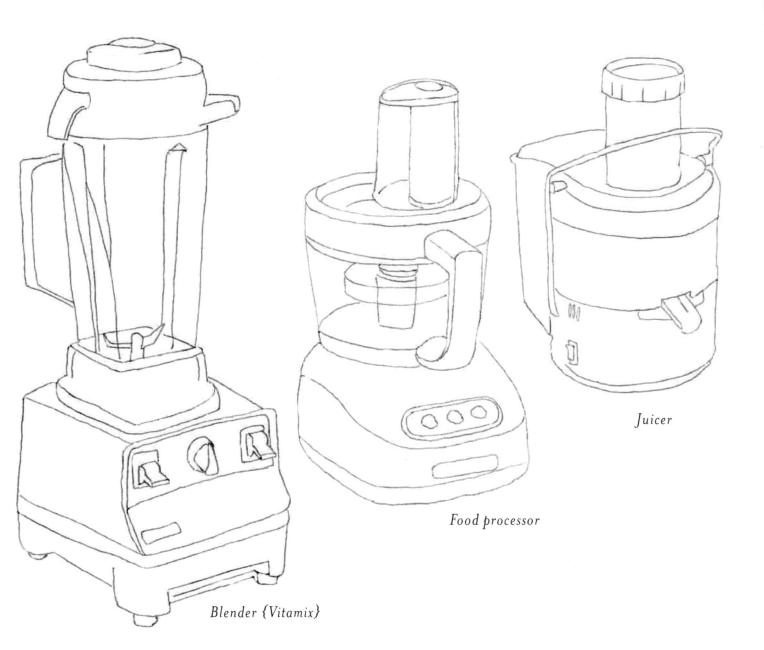

Blender {Vitamix}

Food processor

Juicer

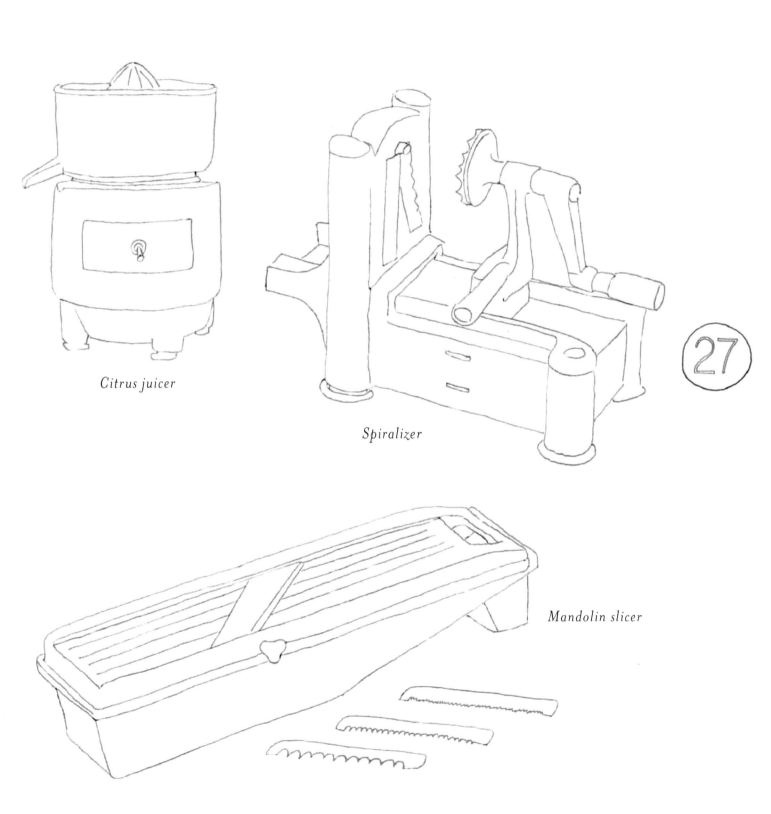

Citrus juicer

Spiralizer

27

Mandolin slicer

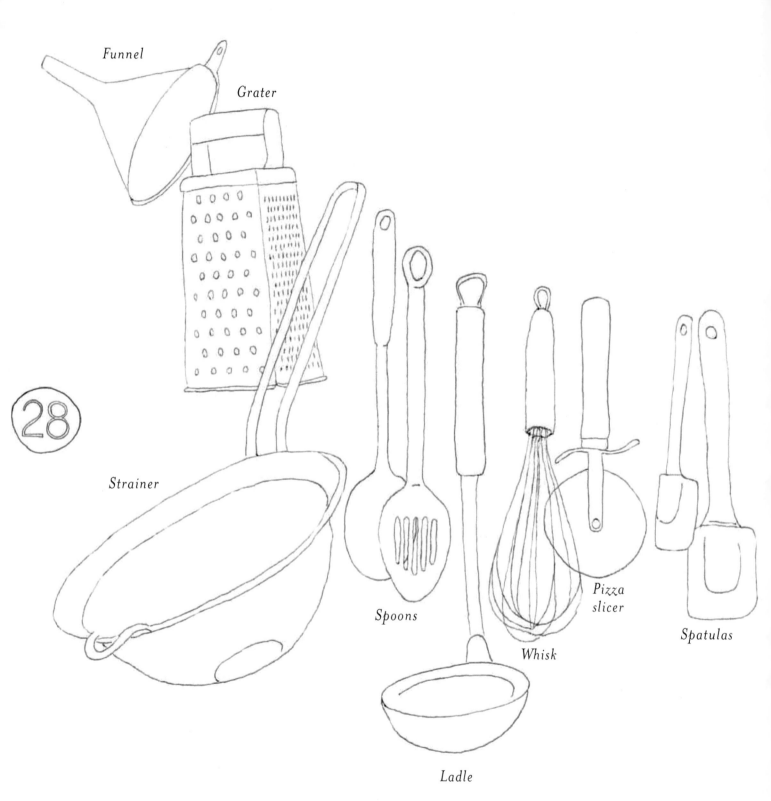

Funnel

Grater

28

Strainer

Spoons

Ladle

Whisk

Pizza slicer

Spatulas

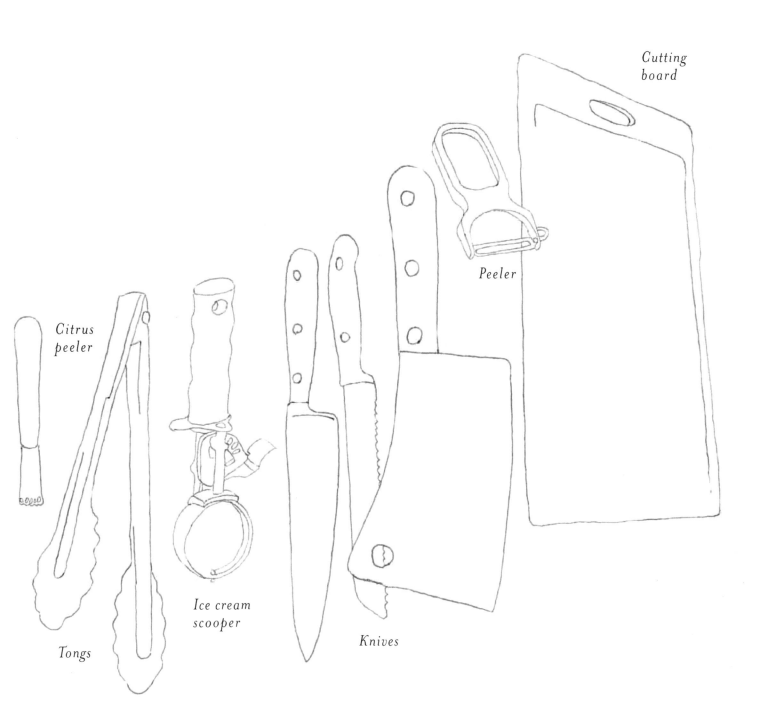

Citrus
peeler

Tongs

Ice cream
scooper

Knives

Peeler

Cutting
board

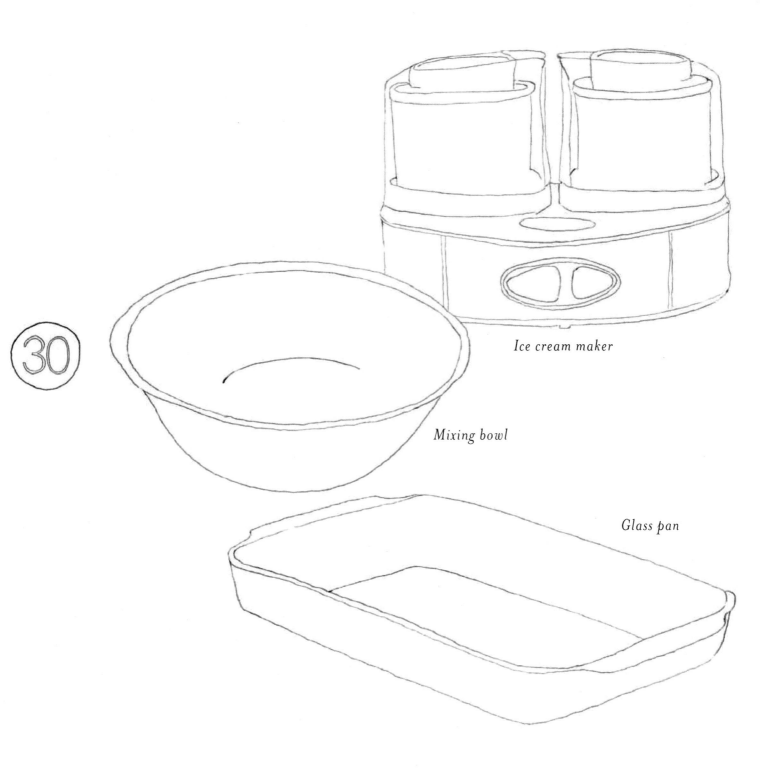

30

Ice cream maker

Mixing bowl

Glass pan

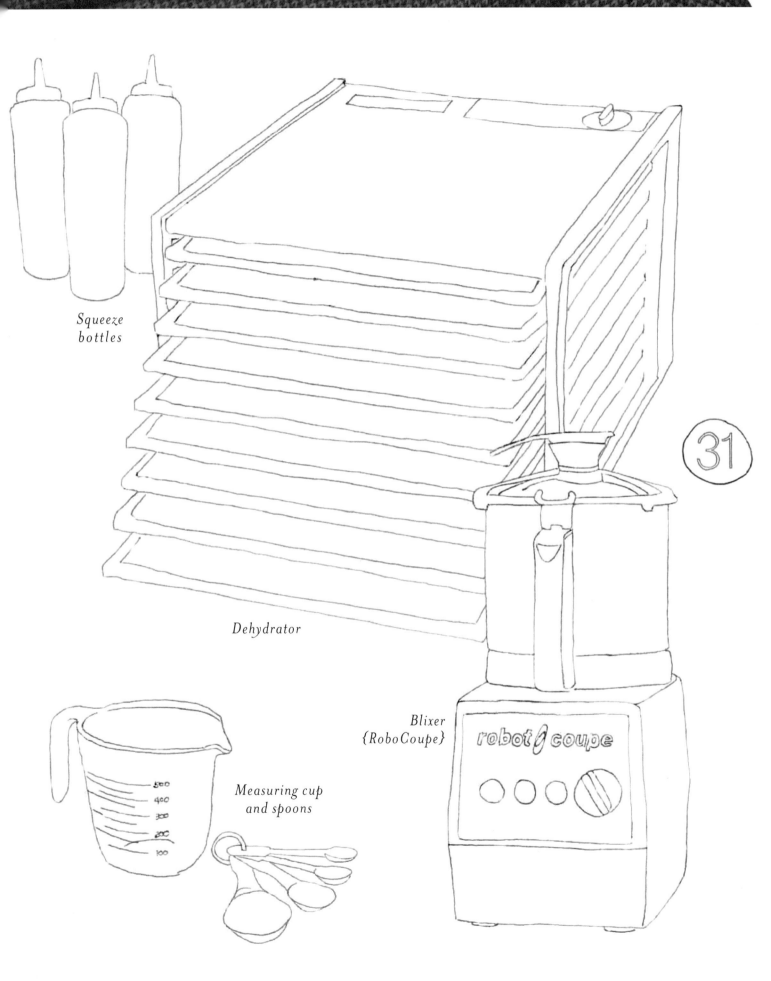

Squeeze
bottles

Dehydrator

Measuring cup
and spoons

Blixer
{RoboCoupe}

robot coupe

31

Present Moment Salad Dressing

yields 2 cups

ingredients

¾ cup lemon juice
¾ cup olive oil
2 Tbsp agave
1 tsp salt
1 tsp white pepper

directions

Pour all ingredients into a squeeze bottle and
shake well. This salad dressing lasts 5 -7 days in fridge.

Cashew Mayonnaise

yields 1 quart

ingredients

3 cups cashews, soaked 1-2 hours
1 cup filtered water
2 cloves garlic
¼ cup olive oil
2 Tbsp lemon juice
3 Tbsp agave
1 Tbsp onion powder
1 tsp salt
½ tsp white pepper

directions

1 Drain and rinse cashews well.
2 In Vitamix, blend all ingredients to a smooth and
   creamy consistency.
3 Taste and adjust salt or water if necessary.

Caramelized Onions

yields 1 quart

ingredients

4 red onions
1/3 cup tamari
1/3 cup olive oil
¾ cup **date paste** {see recipe below}
2 cloves garlic, minced

directions

1 Slice onions paper-thin on a mandoline.
2 In a large mixing bowl, massage together all the above
   ingredients until thouroughly combined.
3 Taste and adjust salt if needed.

Date Paste

yields 2 cups

ingredients

20 pitted dates
Soaked 30 minutes with enough water to cover.

directions

1 In food processor, blend the dates until a smooth
   paste is achieved, adding water as needed.

Pine Nut Parmesan

yields 1 quart

ingredients

4 cups pine nuts
½ cup nutritional yeast
2 ½ Tbsp onion powder
2 Tbsp white miso
2 tsp salt

directions

Pulse all ingredients into crumbles in the food processor, being mindful not to over-process.

Pesto

yields 2 cups

ingredients

2 cups chopped basil
½ cup pine nuts
6 cloves garlic
½ tsp salt
2 Tbsp olive oil

directions

1 In the food processor, gently pulse the basil, pine nuts, garlic, and salt, gradually adding the olive oil.
2 Stop blending when the mixture is fully combined, but still slightly textured.

White Truffle Cream

yields 3 cups

ingredients

1 ½ cups cashews, soaked 1-2 hours
½ cup pine nuts
½ cup filtered water
¼ cup lemon juice
2 Tbsp tamari
2 Tbsp agave
2 Tbsp white truffle oil
pinch white pepper
pinch nutmeg
pinch salt

directions

1 Drain and rinse cashews well.
2 In Vitamix, blend all ingredients to a smooth and creamy consistency.
3 Taste and adjust salt or water if necessary.

Red Pepper Marinara

yields 1 quart

ingredients

4 red bell peppers, seeded and chopped
2 medium chopped tomatoes
1 apple, cored and chopped
5 cloves garlic
1 cup sun dried tomato, soaked for 2-3 hours
1 cup basil, fresh and chopped
¼ cup olive oil
2 Tbsp red wine
2 tsp oregano
2 tsp Italian seasonings
pinch salt
pinch black pepper

directions

Blend all ingredients in Vitamix until smooth.

33

Jalapeño Vinaigrette

yields 1 quart

ingredients

1 ½ cups diced green onion
15 jalapeños, seeded
5 Tbsp garlic, minced
1 bunch cilantro de- stemmed
1 ¼ cups apple cider vinegar
1 cup agave
3 Tbsp cumin powder
1 Tbsp black pepper
½ Tbsp salt
3 cups olive oil

directions

1 Mince green onions, jalapenos, garlic, and cilantro in food processor, careful not to puree.
2 Whisk all ingredients together in a large mixing bowl, slowly adding the olive oil.
3 Using a funnel, pour all ingredients into a squeeze bottle and shake well before use.

Mexican Cheese

yields 2 cups

ingredients

1 ½ cups cashews, soaked 1- 2 hours
1 red bell pepper, seeded and chopped
2 cloves garlic
2 Tbsp nutritional yeast
2 Tbsp olive oil
2 Tbsp filtered water
1 Tbsp tamari
1 Tbsp agave
½ Tbsp lemon juice
1 tsp onion powder
pinch smoked salt

directions

1 Drain and rinse cashews well.
2 In Vitamix, blend all ingredients to a smooth and creamy consistency.
3 Taste and adjust salt or water if necessary.

Cashew Sour Cream

yields 3 cups

ingredients

1 ¾ cups cashews, soaked 1- 2 hours
2/3 cup filtered water
2 Tbsp cup olive oil
1 ½ Tbsp lemon juice
1 ½ Tbsp agave
½ tsp salt

directions

1 Drain and rinse cashews well.
2 In Vitamix, blend all ingredients to a smooth and creamy consistency.
3 Taste and adjust salt or water if necessary.

Shoyu

yields 1 quart

3 cups tamari
½ cup apple cider vinegar
½ cup agave
1/3 cup toasted sesame oil
1/3 cup minced ginger
1/3 cup minced green onions.
3 Tbsp garlic, minced
1 Tbsp jalapenos, seeded and minced

directions

1 Whisk all ingredients together in a large mixing bowl.
2 Using a funnel, pour all ingredients into a squeeze bottle and shake well.

Almond Ginger

yields 1 quart

ingredients

1 cup almond butter
1 cup tamari
1 cup water
½ cup agave
¼ cup sesame oil
¼ cup toasted sesame oil
3 Tbsp lime juice
3 Tbsp ginger, minced
6 cloves garlic, minced

directions

1 In Vitamix, blend all ingredients to a smooth and creamy consistency.
2 Taste and adjust salt or water if necessary.

Pad Thai Sauce

yields 1 quart

ingredients

1 cup cashews, soaked 1- 2 hours
8 cloves garlic
½ cup sesame oil
½ cup tamari
½ cup filtered water
2 Tbsp maple syrup
½ tsp crushed red pepper

directions

1 Drain and rinse cashews well.
2 In Vitamix, blend all ingredients to a smooth and creamy consistency.
3 Taste and adjust salt or water if necessary.

Mint Coulis

yields 2 cups

ingredients

1/4 cup raisins, soaked in 1/2 cup water until tender
1 cup packed mint leaves
1/3 cups cilantro de-stemmed
1/4 cup olive oil
1 Tbsp lemon juice
1/4 tsp salt

directions

1 Strain raisins reserving soak water.
2 In Vitamix, blend all ingredients to a smooth and creamy consistency, using the raisin water.
3 Using a funnel, pour all ingredients into squeeze bottles and shake well.

Berry Coulis

yields 1 cup

ingredients

1 cup strawberries, blueberries, or berries of your choice
1 Tbsp agave
2 tsp lemon juice
pinch cinnamon
pinch salt

directions

1 Blend all ingredients until smooth and creamy.
2 Taste and adjust salt or add water to thin if necessary.

why soak nuts?

Enzyme inhibitors are released in the soaking process, making them more digestible and more nutritionally beneficial. When soaking nuts, always remember to rinse and drain well before including in recipes.

Rum Sauce

yields 2 cups

1 cup agave
½ cup rum of your choice
¼ cup maple syrup
½ Tbsp vanilla

Using a funnel, pour all ingredients into a squeeze bottle and shake well..

Vanilla Crème

yields 3 cups

1 ½ cups cashews, soaked 1- 2 hours
¾ cup filtered water
½ cup coconut meat
½ cup agave
½ Tbsp vanilla
½ tsp salt

1 Drain and rinse cashews well.
2 In Vitamix, blend all ingredients to a smooth and creamy consistency.
3 Taste and adjust agave or water if necessary.

Cacao Sauce

yields 2 cups

2 cups cacao powder
1 cup filtered water
½ cup agave
¼ cup maple syrup
1 tsp tamari
1 tsp vanilla
½ tsp lemon juice
pinch salt

1 In Vitamix, blend all ingredients to a smooth and creamy consistency.
2 Taste and adjust agave or water if necessary.

Cashew hummus

Hummus

yields 1 quart

ingredients

3 cups cashews, soaked 1- 2 hours
½ cup lemon juice
½ cup filtered water
¼ cup tahini
¼ cup olive oil
7 cloves garlic
1 ½ Tbsp cumin powder
1 tsp salt

directions

1 Drain and rinse cashews well.
2 Blend all ingredients in Vitamix until smooth and creamy.
3 Serve garnished with **mint coulis**
{see recipe page 36}

Spinach Dip

yields 1 quart

ingredients

2 pounds frozen spinach, thawed
½ cup olive oil
¼ cup pine nuts
¼ cup white miso
¼ cup nutritional yeast
6 cloves of garlic
2 Tbsp lemon juice
¾ Tbsp agave
½ tsp salt

directions

1 Squeeze out all liquid from the thawed spinach and set aside.
2 Combine all ingredients except for the spinach in a food processor.
3 Gently pulse the spinach into the sauce a little bit at a time being mindful not to over-process. Dip should have a slightly textured consistency.

cashews

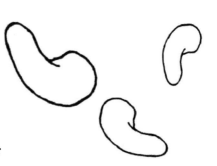

Cashew nuts are loaded with "good" fats and are a rich source of phytochemicals and antioxidants. These chemicals are believed by many to protect against cancer and heart disease.

Guacamole

yields 1 quart

ingredients

8 avocados, seeded and chopped
8 cloves garlic, minced
¼ cup diced red onion
½ cup chopped cilantro
3 Tbsp lime juice
1 tsp salt

directions

1 Combine all ingredients in a large mixing bowl.
2 With gloved hands, mash the avocado into tiny chunks, being mindful to completely blend all ingredients.

Salsa

yields 1 quart

ingredients

3 cups of seeded and diced tomatoes (setting seeds & pulp aside)
½ bunch chopped cilantro
3 cloves garlic, minced
½ cup sundried tomatoes, soaked 2- 3 hours
¼ cup diced red onion
¼ cup diced green onion
1 ½ Tbsp apple cider vinegar
1 tsp salt

directions

1 In a medium sized bowl combine diced tomatos, cilantro, red and green onion, vinegar and salt.
2 In the Vitamix, combine the tomato seeds and pulp with the drained sundried tomatoes into a smooth paste.
3 Gently stir the tomato sauce into the diced veggies.

Chips

*yields 10 trays
{320 chips}*

ingredients

5 cups flax seeds, soaked 2- 4 hours in enough water to cover
5 cups almonds, soaked 10-12 hours
3 pounds corn (fresh or frozen, organic, non GMO)*
6 yellow bell peppers, seeded and chopped
1 red bell pepper, seeded and chopped
¾ cup onion powder
5 Tbsp dried oregano
3 Tbsp cumin
¾ tsp salt

directions

1 Drain and rinse almonds well and simply drain the flax seeds
2 In a large mixing bowl, thouroughly mix all ingredients.
3 Blend about 3 cups of the mixture at a time in Vitamix until smooth and creamy, continously transfering the batter to a large mixing bowl.
4 Mix all the batter by hand.
5 On teflex and mesh lined dehydrator sheets, spread about 2½ cups of batter on evenly with a spatula.
6 Score into 32 even-sized chips. {see photo}
7 Place trays in dehydrator at 115 degrees overnight.
8 Flip the chips by placing a second mesh lined dehydrator tray face down on the chips. Grab the two trays along the side and flip over. Then remove the top tray and peel away the teflex sheet. Return chips to dehydrator for 8 hours or until crisp.

*GMO- Genetically Modified Organism

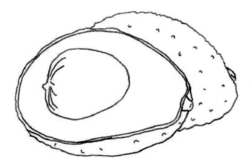

avocado

Always cut the stem off the avocado first, or you may end up serving it to your guest!

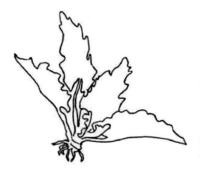

vegan calcium

The most healthful calcium sources are green leafy vegetables, in particular spring greens, kale, broccoli, and parsley.

42

kelp noodle

Kelp is called a "miracle plant" because of its many therapeutic properties. Kelp is known to aid metabolism, promote weight loss, boost energy, aid in digestion.

why raw?

Benefits of eating raw include improved skin appearance, weight loss, reduced risk of heart disease, cancer, and diabetes, anti-aging and renewed enthusiasm for life!

Kale Chips

yields 1 quart

ingredients

6 bunches kale
½ cup tamari
½ cup agave
¼ cup sesame oil
¼ cup toasted sesame oil
2 Tbsp garlic powder
2 Tbsp onion powder
2 Tbsp lime juice
2 tsp chili powder
½ tsp salt

directions

1 De-stem, rinse, and dry the kale.
2 Blend all ingredients, except for kale until smooth.
3 Drizzle each leaf of kale with the sauce until the leaf is coated but not saturated.
4 Place on teflex and mesh lined dehydrator trays.
5 Dehydrate at 120 degrees for 10- 12 hours.
6 Remove teflex sheet and dehydrate at 120 degrees for an additional hour or until crisp.

Spring Rolls

yields 10 rolls

ingredients

filling:
10 rice paper wrappers
2 carrots peeled
2 avocados, pitted
1 red bell pepper
¼ head cabbage
2 cups mung bean sprouts
1 cup fresh spinach
1 cup cilantro, chopped
1 cup mint, chopped
1 cup thai basil, chopped

sauce:
2 cups sesame oil
1 cup filtered water
½ cup agave
¼ cup tamari
3 Tbsp minced ginger
1 Tbsp toasted sesame oil
1 Tbsp apple cider vinegar
8 cloves garlic
½ tsp salt
pinch of red pepper flakes

directions

1 Thinly slice carrots, cabbage, bell peppers, spinach, and avocado.
2 Soak one rice paper wrapper at a time in luke warm water for 10 to 20 seconds. Move to clean cutting board. {Do not soak longer or it will fall apart}
3 Immediately after the wrapper has been soaked, place 2 Tbl of **filling** ingredients into the center and wrap it up, folding over itself and sealing the ends. Repeat for each.
4 Blend **sauce** ingredients in Vita Mix until smooth and creamy.
5 Serve the spring rolls and sauce together.

43

Sea Veggies

yields 1 quarts

ingredients

2 cups arame
½ cup **shoyu sauce**
 {see recipe page 35}
¼ cup fresh lime juice
2 Tbsp diced green onions
2 Tbsp diced red pepper
2 Tbsp thinly sliced carrots
2 Tbsp white sesame seeds

directions

1 Soak arame for 30 minutes. Strain, squeezing out all the excess water.
2 Combine all ingredients in large mixing bowl and toss well.

Crab Cakes

yields 8 crab cakes

ingredients

1 cup coconut meat, cleaned and chopped
1 cups corn meal
¼ cup diced red pepper
¼ cup diced celery
2 Tbsp chopped parsley
1 Tbsp **cashew mayonaisse**
 {see recipe page 32}
½ Tbsp old bay seasoning

directions

1 Crack coconuts open with a large, heavy knife. Scoop the meat out with a spoon. To clean, use a small knife to remove all brown pithy pieces from the white meat.
2 Grind corn meal in a coffee grinder or Vitamix. Sift corn meal twice.
3 Pulse all ingredients except cornmeal in food processor.
4 Transfer the mixture to a large mixing bowl and add ½ cup of the corn meal to bind the batter together.
5 Chill for 30 minutes in the refrigerator.
6 Use an ice cream scoop to create batter balls and dip each ball into the remaining cornmeal, coating all sides.
7 Form the balls into flattened patties, placing them on teflex and mesh lined dehydrator trays.
8 Dehydrate for 2 hours at 125 degrees.
9 Flip the patties off of the teflex, dehyrate another hour.

44

arame

Arame is highly rich in essential nutrients including calcium, iron, zinc, manganese, folate, vitamins A & K, and iodine. Arame also provides immune system support and healthier hair, skin, and nails.

Sea Veggies

45

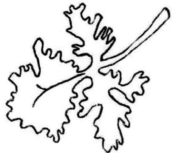

cilantro

The chemical compounds in cilantro bind to heavy metals, loosening them from the tissues, blood and organs, then transporting these harmful substances out of the body through elimination.

no GMO!

We consciously do not purchase genetically modified corn or soybeans. Resist the commodification of life. Resist biotechnology.

46

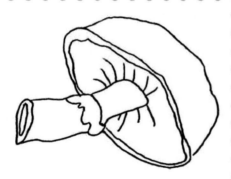

shiitake

The basis of the shiitake mushroom's impressive health properties are complex carbohydrates called polysaccharides that build the immune system.

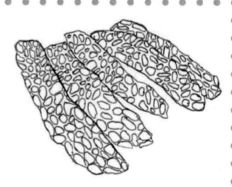

tempeh

Tempeh is a complete soy protein food that contains Isoflavones, which strengthen bones, help to ease menopause symptoms, and reduce risk of coronary heart disease.

Jalapeño Poppers

serves 10

ingredients

1 pound jalapeños
1 quart **mexican cheese**
{see recipe page 34}
10 lime slices
20 cilantro leaves

directions

1 Wearing gloves, cut the jalapeños in half, removing all
   seeds and veins.
2 Use a squeeze bottle to fill each pepper slice with
   mexican cheese. Cut tip off squeeze bottle for easy appliction.
3 Place peppers in dehydrator on 125 for minimum of six hour.
   The longer you dehydrate the softer the peppers become and crisper the cheese.

Chili Rellenos

serves 10

ingredients

10 red bell peppers
1 quart **taco pâté**
{see recipe page 60}
1 cup **mexican cheese**
{see recipe page 34}
2 Tbsp diced green onion

directions

1 Cut each pepper into 4 slices, removing seeds and veins.
2 Fill each pepper slice with a scoop of **taco pâté**   .
3 Place peppers in dehydrator on 125 for one hour.
4 Remove peppers from dehydrator and use a squeeze
   bottle to drizzle **mexican cheese** over each.
5 Dehydrate for an additional hour or longer to taste.
6 Serve garnished with diced green onion.

47

sprouts

Sprouts like alfalfa, radish, broccoli, clover and soybean contain concentrated amounts of phytochemicals (plant compounds) that protect against disease.

Miso

serves 4

ingredients

base:
2 cups coconut water
1 cup white miso
1 cup hot water

vegetables:
1 Tbsp shitake mushrooms sliced thin
1 Tbsp coconut meat cut into noodles
1 Tbsp diced green onions
1 Tbsp diced red bell pepper
1 Tbsp shredded nori
1 tsp sesame seeds

directions

1 In Vitamix, blend **base** ingredients to smooth consistency.
2 Pour into soup pan.
3 Stir in remaining **vegetables.**

Chili

yields 1 quart

ingredients

base:
1 cup sundried tomatoes
2 cup filtered water
1 cup sundried tomato water
1 chopped tomato
½ bunch chopped cilantro
½ jalapeno - seeded
1 Tbsp lime juice
1 Tbsp onion powder
1 Tbsp chili powder
1 Tbsp cumin powder
1 Tbsp agave
½ Tbsp thyme
½ Tbsp garlic powder
½ Tbsp black pepper

vegetables:
1 cup corn
¼ cup diced green onion
¼ cup diced red onion
½ cup diced red bell pepper
½ cup **taco paté**
  {see recipe page 60}

directions

1 Soak sundied tomatoes 30 minutes. When soft, drain but
  save the water for the recipe.
2 In Vitamix, blend **base** ingredients to smooth consistency.
2 Pour into soup pan.
3 Add the remaining **vegetables** and mix well.
4 Serve garnished with **sour cream** and **mexican cheese**
  {see recipes page 34}

Broccoli Cheddar

yields 1 quart

ingredients

base:
3 cups filtered water
2 cups cashews,
    soaked 1- 2 hours
1 seeded red bell pepper
¼ cup nutritional yeast
¼ cup olive oil
2 cloves of garlic
1 Tbsp onion powder
1 Tbsp tamari
1 Tbsp agave
½ tsp salt
¼ tsp white pepper

vegetables:
1 ½ cups broccoli florets cut
  into small pieces.

directions

1 Drain and rinse cashews well.
2 In Vita-mix, blend **base** ingredients to smooth consistency.
3 Pour into soup pan.
4 Add broccoli to the soup.

Southwest Corn Chowder

serves 4

ingredients

base:
¾ cup cashews,
    soaked 1- 2 hours
3 cups corn
¾ cup pine nuts
3 cloves garlic
½ jalapeño, seeded
1 Tbsp onion powder
1 Tbsp chili powder
1 Tbsp cumin powder
1 Tbsp agave
1 tsp salt

vegetables:
1 cup corn
1 cup diced tomatoes
½ cup diced red bell pepper
¼ cup diced red onion
¼ cup diced green onion
¼ cup chopped c ilantro

directions

1 Drain and rinse cashews well.
2 In Vitamix, blend **base** ingredients to smooth consistency.
3 Pour into soup pan.
4 Stir in the remaining **vegetables.**
5 Serve garnished with **sour cream** and **mexican cheese**
    {see recipes page 34}

Tom Kha Gai

yields 1 quart

ingredients

4 cups coconut milk {see recipe page 82}
½ cup diced green onion
1 Tbsp light miso
1 Tbsp lime juice
1 Tbsp red curry paste
1 Tbsp green curry paste
1 Tbsp agave
1 Tbsp tamari
2 cloves garlic
½ tsp salt

directions

1 In Vitamix, blend **base** ingredients to smooth consistency.
2 Pour into soup pan.
3 Add **marinated asian vegetables** to the base.
    {see recipe page 68}

Pineapple Cucumber Gazpacho

yields 1½ quarts

ingredients

base:
2 cups peeled cucumbers
2 cups peeled pinapple
¼ cup chopped cilantro
1 Tbsp minced jalapeno
1 Tbsp minced scallions
1 Tbsp olive oil
1 Tbsp lime juice
½ tsp salt

vegetables:
½ cup peeled and diced cucumber
½ cup peeled and diced pineapple
½ cup dry macadamia nuts
¼ cup diced scallions
¼ cup chopped cilantro

directions

1 In Vitamix, blend **base** ingredients to smooth consistency.
2 Pour into soup pan.
3 Pulse **vegetables** including macadamia nuts in food processor
    until chopped. Add this to the soup base.
4 Serve chilled, garnished with lime slice.

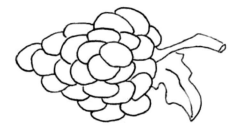

fermentation

Fermented vegetables are made with lactic acid bacteria, which is a valuable technique humans have been using for thousands of years.

miso

Miso is a fermented soybean paste that has been a mainstay of Japanese cooking for hundreds of years. It contains all essential amino acids, making it a perfect protein.

51

coconut

Coconut water has a powerhouse of anti aging properties to help keep you looking younger, with more electrolytes than Gatorade!

why raw?

Eating vegetables in their raw state will ensure you get all the vitamins they contain. Live enzymes die at 118° F.

garlic

Raw garlic is an anti-fungal agent, a powerful antibiotic, and benefits the cardiovascular system. Garlic is also widely believed to prevent certain types of cancer, including stomach and colon cancers.

lobster mushroom

This mushroom has a unique growth process - it actually eats other mushrooms, deriving nutrients from them. Lobster mushrooms provide protein, fiber, a substantial amount of B vitamins, and copper.

52

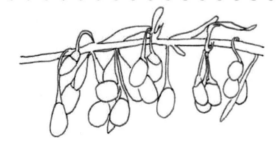

goji berries

People have used goji berries to treat many common health problems like diabetes, high blood pressure, fever, and age-related eye problems. Some claim that goji berries are the next fountain of youth!

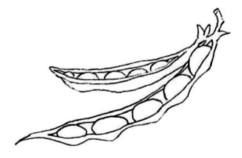

no GMO!

We consciously do not purchase genetically modified corn or soybeans. Resist the commodification of life. Resist biotechnology.

Potato Leek

yields 1 quart

ingredients

base:
1 cup dehydrated potato
3 cups water
1 cup soaked cashews
1 Tbsp olive oil
1 Tbsp pine nuts
1 Tbsp tamari
1 Tbsp agave
1 Tbsp nutritional yeast
1 Tbsp onion powder
1 Tbsp garlic powder
½ tsp white pepper

vegetables:
1 cup diced leeks
½ cup diced green onion

directions

1 Soak dehydrated potato until soft and tender.
  This will double in size when soaked.
2 In the Vitamix, combine **base** ingredients until smooth and
  creamy. Water may be continually added for consistency.
3 Add **vegetables** to the **base** and mix well.

Lobster Mushroom Bisque

yields 1 quart

ingredients

base:
2½ cups water
1 cup soaked cashews
1 Tbsp olive oil
1 Tbsp sherry wine
1 Tbsp onion powder
½ Tbsp garlic powder
½ Tbsp old bay seasoning
½ tsp black pepper
½ tsp salt

vegetables:
½ cup soaked lobster mushrooms
½ cup diced coconut meat

directions

1 Blend base ingredients in Vitamix until smooth and creamy.
2 Drain lobster mushrooms and pulse in food processor to mince.
3 Add diced coconut meat and mushrooms to **base**.
4 Serve slightly warm, garnished with a lemon wedge.

53

Carrot Ginger

yields 1 quart

ingredients

base:
4 carrots
1 inches ginger
2 cups coconut water
1 Tbsp sesame oil
1 Tbsp tamari
1 Tbsp agave
1 Tbsp lime juice
½ Tbsp garlic powder

vegetables:
1/4 cup diced green onion
1/4 cup finely sliced carrot
1/4 cup diced yellow bell pepper

directions

1 Juice the carrot and ginger in a juicer.
2 In the Vitamix, combine **base** ingredients with the juice.
3 Add the **vegetables** to the base.

SALADS

Kale ala Present Moment

serves 4

ingredients

1 head of kale
1 avocado, pitted and diced
½ cup diced red bell pepper
½ cup diced red onion
½ cup diced green onion
½ cup **lemon oil**
  {see recipe page 32}
2 Tbsp sesame seeds
½ tsp salt
½ tsp cayenne

directions

1 Thoroughly wash and dry kale, remove stems, cut into bit size pieces.
2 Combine all ingredients in large mixing bowl, squeezing
  as you mix to 'wilt' the kale and cream the avocado.
3 Serve garnished with sprouts and **candied pecans**
  {see recipe page 79}

Crown of Caesar

serves 4

ingredients

salad
2 heads romaine lettuce
½ cup dulse seaweed

dressing
5 stalks of celery, chopped
8 pitted dates
6 cloves garlic
1 cup olive oil
½ cup water
¼ cup tamari
¼ cup kelp granules
½ cup lemon juice
3 Tbsp white miso
1 tsp salt

directions

1 Thoroughly wash and dry romaine, shred, and toss with dulse.
2 In Vitamix, blend **dressing** ingredients until smooth and creamy.
3 Toss **salad** with the **dressing** and sprinkle on **rosemary garlic croutons** {recipe this page}

55

Rosemary Garlic Croutons

yields 3 trays
{for use with Caesar salad}

ingredients

2 cups flax, soaked 4-6 hours
2 cups almonds, soaked 6-8 hours
3 carrots, chopped
2 cups chopped celery
1 cup chopped red bell pepper
3 Tbsp dried rosemary
2 Tbsp garlic powder
2 Tbsp dried Italian seasoning
1 Tbsp salt

directions

1 Drain and rinse almonds well.
2 Combine all ingredients in a large mixing bowl, stir well.
3 Blend about 3 cups of batter at a time in the food processor.
4 Transfer the smooth batter into a large mixing bowl, stir well.
5 On teflex and mesh lined dehydrator trays, spread a ½ inch
  thick layer onto each tray, spreading evenly with a spatula.
6 Score into 20x20 croutons.
7 Place in a dehydrator at 115 degrees overnight.

Tabouli

yields 1 quart

ingredients

5 seeded and diced tomatoes
3 seeded and diced cucumbers
1 diced red bell peppers
½ diced red onion
4 cloves garlic
1 bunch flat parsley, stems removed and chopped fine
1 bunch curly parsley, stems removed and chopped fine
1 bunch mint, finely chopped
½ cup lemon juice
½ cup olive oil
½ tsp salt
½ tsp black pepper

directions

1 In a blender add garlic, lemon juice, olive oil, salt and pepper.
2 Pour over diced veggies and marinate in fridge to chill.

Un-Tuna Salad

yields ½ quart

ingredients

2 ½ cups sunflower seeds, soaked 10-12 hours
½ cup almonds, soaked 10-12 hours
½ cup diced celery
½ cup diced red onion
½ cup diced pickles
¼ cup lemon juice
1 ½ Tbsp kelp granules
1 ½ Tbsp olive oil
1 Tbsp dry dill
1 Tbsp agave
1 tsp salt
½ tsp black pepper

directions

1 Drain and rinse sunflower seeds and almonds well.
2 Homogenize the sunflower seeds and almonds in food processor to a smooth paste.
3 In a large mixing bowl, add the remaining ingredients and mix thouroughly with a spatula.
4 Serve alone or over mixed greens, garnish with lemon.

Guac, salsa and chips

Entrées

Collard Wrap

yields 1 wrap

ingredients

1 large collard leaf
2 Tbsp **hummus**
   {see recipe page 39}
1 red bell pepper
1 avocado
1 carrot
1 cucumber
1 mango
1 celery stalk
¼ head of red cabbage
½ cup clover sprouts

directions

1 Slice vertically against the stem of a single collard leaf to create a flat, pliable wrapper.
2 Spread the **hummus** evenly onto the collard leaf.
3 Slice all vegetables into long, thin strips. Use 2- 4 slices of each veggie in a wrap.
4 Layer the ingredients variably, creating a rainbow of color, and stacking in the center.
5 Pull the left and right sides of the collard leaf over the filling, and roll tightly, like a burrito.
6 • OPTIONAL • For added stability, you may roll plastic wrap around the collard
7 Serve wrap sliced in half, with **almond ginger sauce** {see recipe page 35} and **chips** {see recipe page 40}.

59

zucchini noodles

Spiralizing fresh zucchinis creates our signature pastas. The vegetable proves to be a good source of magnesium and phosphorus, the nutrients essential for building and maintaining healthy bones.

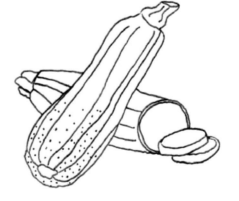

Nutmeat

yields 1 ¼ quarts

ingredients

2 cups diced portabella mushrooms
¼ cup tamari
1 ½ cups walnuts, soaked 10-12 hours
1 ½ cups almonds, soaked 10-12 hours
1 ½ cups sunflower seeds, soaked 10-12 hours
1 Tbsp garlic, minced
1 stalk celery, diced
½ cup grated zucchini
½ cup grated carrots
¼ cup diced red onion
½ Tbsp cumin powder
½ tsp minced ginger
½ tsp chili powder
½ tsp salt

directions

1 Marinate diced mushrooms in ¼ cup tamari for 30 minutes.
2 In the food processor, homogenize the sunflower seeds, almonds and walnuts into a paste.
3 Transfer to a large mixing bowl and combine with all the remaining ingredients. Taste and adjust salt if necessary.
4 This is our version of ground meat.

serving suggestions

SUNLIGHT BURGER
Form nutmeat into round patties and dehydration on teflex sheet at 125 for 3 hours. Flip and dehydrate for another hour. Serve burger over a bed of sprouts, garnished with a slice of tomato, **cashew mayo** {see recipe page 32}, **carmelized onions** {see recipe page 32}, and fresh pickle.

HERBED NUTLOAF / PORTABELLA CROQUETTES
Form nutmeat into square loaf for nutloaf or small round balls for croquettes. Dehydrate 4- 5 hours for nutloaf or 2- 3 hours for croquettes. Serve with **marinara sauce** {see recipe page 33} and sprinkle with **pine nut parmesan** {see recipe page 33}.

Tacos of Life

yields 6 tacos

ingredients

pâté
3 cups walnuts,
   soaked 10-12 hours
1 cup pine nuts
½ cup diced tomato
½ cup corn
½ cup diced green onion
¼ cup minced cilantro
¼ cup minced basil
¼ cup dark miso
2 Tbsp chili powder
1 Tbsp cumin powder
½ tsp salt

toppings
1 head romaine lettuce
½ cup **guacamole**
   {see recipe page 42}
½ cup **salsa**
   {see recipe page 42}
½ cup **cashew sour cream**
   {see recipe page 34}
½ cup **mexican cheese**
   {see recipe page 34}
2 Tbsp **jalapeño vinaigrette**
   {see recipe page 34}

directions

1 Drain and rinse nuts.
2 Homogenize nuts in a food processor to a smooth paste.
3 Transfer to a large mixing bowl and fold in the remaining **pâté**
4 To assemble tacos, place individual romaine leafs face up. Place a tablespoon full of pate, guacamole and salsa in your romaine shell.
5 **Toppings**; cashew sour cream, mexican cheese and jalapeno vinaigrette.

Tacos of life

Pasta

yields 1 quart

ingredients

4 zucchinis

directions

1 Peel and cut the ends off zucchini.
2 Use a spiralizer to turn zucchini into pasta.

serving suggestions

PASTA MARINARA
Combine 1 cup zucchini pasta with 1 Tbsp **red pepper marinara** {see recipe page 33}. Dehydrate on 120 for 10 minutes. Serve sprinkled with **pinenut parmesan** {see recipe page 33}.

CREAMY WHITE TRUFFLE PESTO PASTA
Combine 2 cups zucchini pasta to 1 Tbsp **white truffle cream** {see recipe page 33} and 1 Tbsp **pesto** {see recipe page 33}. Dehydrate on 120 for 10 minutes. Serve garnished with diced green onions and sundried tomatoes.

SKYLINE CHILI BOWL
Cover 1 bowl of pasta with **chili** {see recipe page 49}.

Lasagne

yields 12 servings

ingredients

noodles
4 zucchinis

cheese
4 cups soaked cashews
1 cup water
½ cup pine nuts
2 Tbsp nutritional yeast
1 Tbsp onion powder
1 Tbsp olive oil
1½ Tbsp lemon juice

marinade
1 cup olive oil
½ cup nama shoyu
½ cup garlic powder
2 Tbsp lemon juice
2 Tbsp oregano
½ Tbsp salt

vegetables
6 cups fresh spinach, chopped
4 cups crimini mushrooms, diced
4 cups broccoli florets
2 cups basil, chopped

directions

1 Peel and remove ends of zucchinis. Slice thin on a mandolin.
2 In a large mixing bowl, coat zucchini noodles in the **marinade** and let sit for at least 2 hours.
3 Remove noodles from marinade. Re-use the marinade to soak the **vegetables**.
4 In blender, combine all **cheese** ingredients until smooth.
5 In 9" x 13" glass dish; place one layer of noodles, one layer of cheese, one layer of vegetables and another layer of noodles. Top with **red pepper marinara** {see recipe page 33}.
6 • OPTIONAL • Place tomato slices and herbs on top of the lasagne.
7 Place in dehydrator at 120 degrees Fahrenheit for 2 hours.

Stuffed Portabella

yields 4 servings

ingredients

1 ½ Tbsp olive oil
1 ½ Tbsp tamari
1 ½ Tbsp **date paste** {see recipe page 32}
4 portabella mushrooms, stems removed
1 cup **spinach dip** {see recipe page 41}
4 Tbsp **caramelized onions** {see recipe page 32}

directions

1 To make marinade, combine olive oil, tamari, and date paste in blender.
2 In an 8"x8" glass dish, marinade the mushroom caps for 30 mins.
3 Stuff **spinach dip** into each mushroom cap.
4 Top each mushroom with 1 Tbsp **caramelized onions**.
5 Dehydrate for 30 minutes at 125 degrees Fahrenheit.

Sushi Rice

yields 2 cups
{for use with Maki Roll}

ingredients

1 ¼ cups chopped parsnips
¼ cup pine nuts
½ Tbsp sesame oil
½ tsp toasted sesame oil
 1 tsp rice wine vinegar
¾ minced green onion
½ tsp salt
½ tsp black pepper

directions

1 In food processor, pulse all ingredients until minced.
  Be mindful not to over-process. The mixture
  should have white rice consistency.
2 Taste and adjust salt if necessary.

Maki Roll

yields 1 sushi roll

ingredients

1 nori sheet
2 Tbsp **sushi rice**
  {see recipe this page}
1 carrot, thinly sliced
1 cucumber, thinly sliced
1 avocado, thinly sliced
1 Tbsp clover sprouts
1 pinch wasabi paste

directions

1 Lay a nori sheet shiny side down on bamboo rolling mat.
2 Spread 2 Tbsp **sushi rice** evenly across the bottom
  1/3 of the sheet.
3 Assemble with assorted listed vegetables, stacking in the
  center. For best results, keep vegetables neatly arranged.
4 Using the sushi rolling mat, tuck the bottom of the nori
  sheet over ingredients, then roll, leaving an inch at the top.
5 Moisten the top of the nori sheet to ensure a tight seal,
  then complete the roll.
6 Slice into 7 even pieces. For best results, use a very sharp,
  slightly wet knife.
7 Serve with **wasabi sauce** {see recipe below} and **shoyu
  sauce** {see recipe page 35}. Garnish with pickled ginger.

Wasabi Sauce

yields 1 cup
{for use with Maki Roll}

ingredients

½ cup soaked cashews
1 Tbsp olive oil
1 Tbsp wasabi powder
1 Tbsp sesame oil
1 tsp minced ginger
1 tsp lemon juice
1 tsp agave nectar
1 clove garlic
1 pinch sea salt

directions

1 Drain and rinse cashews well.
2 Combine all ingredients in blender until smooth with ¼ cup water.

Maki roll

Chicago-Ian Style Pizza

yields 2 - 10" pizzas

ingredients

crust
1 pint of grape tomatoes
½ cup sundried tomatoe water
4 sundried tomatoes
1 Tbsp minced garlic
½ Tbsp salt
1 tsp dry basil
2 cups ground flax
2 cup sunflower seeds

sauce
2 cups soaked sundried tomatoes
1 Tbsp ground fennel
1 clove garlic
½ Tbsp onion powder
1 Tbsp Italian seasoning
½ cup of sundried tomatoe water
1 Tbsp olive oil

cheese
{see Lasagna recipe page 63}

toppings
1 cup fresh chopped spinach
1/3 cup pitted olives
2 Tbsp diced crimini mushrooms
2 Tbsp diced red bell pepper
2 Tbsp diced red onion
1 Tbsp **pinenut parmesan**
   {see recipe page 33}
1/4 chopped fresh basil

directions

crust

1 In food processor, grind sunflower seeds and flax to a flour.
2 Place flour into a mixing bowl and add to it garlic, salt and basil.
3 In a food processor mix the grape and sundried tomatoes into a paste.
4 Fold the paste into the flour mixture.
5 Place all in batches into the food processor until it appears as a whole grain dough.
6 On a teflex sheet roll out dough with rolling pin into a 10" crust.
7 Flip onto another teflex sheet and re-roll. To prevent sticking use wet hands.
8 Remove top teflex sheet and dehydrate crust for 12 hours at 115 degrees. Then flip the crust and dehydrate for another 12 hours.

sauce

Blend all sauce ingredients in Vitamix until smooth and creamy.

pizza

1 Use a spatula to spread a thin, even layer of **sauce** over the dehydrated crust.
2 Gently spread the **cheese** over the **sauce**.
3 Place the **toppings** over the pizza.
4 Sprinkle additonal **pinenut parmesan** over the vegetables.
5 Dehydrate pizza for 2 hours at 115 degrees.

Asian Patty

yields 9 patties

4 carrots
3 zucchinis
4 red bell peppers
4 celery stalks
1 red onion
½ head red cabbage
1 cup nama shoyu
1 cup olive oil
¼ cup agave
¼ cup black sesame seeds
1 Tbsp crushed garlic
1 Tbsp toasted sesame oil
2 tsp chili powder
1 tsp cayenne
1 tsp apple cider vinegar
¼ tsp white pepper
¼ cup tomato powder concentrate

directions

1 Peel carrots and zucchinis and slice all vegetables
  into thin strips using a mandolin.
2 Combine all ingredients except tomato powder in a
  large mixing bowl.
3 Place into a 9"x13" glass pan and dehydrate for 2 hours at
  120 degrees.
4 Combine the mixture in a food processor, being
  mindful not to over-process, while slowly adding
  the tomato powder.
5 Form mixture into patties.
6 Dehydrate on teflex-lined dehydrator sheets for 2
  hours at 120 degrees.

Pad Thai

yields 1 quart

ingredients

½ pound kelp noodles

marinade
2 Tbsp tamari
2 Tbsp sesame oil
1 Tbsp agave

vegetables
½ cup chopped bok choy
¼ cup snow peas
¼ thinly sliced red bell pepper
¼ cup broccoli florets
¼ cup thinly sliced carrot

directions

1 Soak kelp noodles for one hour in 1qt water + 1 tsp
  aluminum free baking soda. Drain and rinse well.
2 Soak kelp noodles in half of the **marinade**.
3 In a medium sized mixing bowl, combine **vegetables**
  with remaining half of the **marinade**, coating thoroughly.
4 In each bowl, place a 4 ounce portion of kelp noodles,
  topped with a scoop of marinated vegetables.
5 Dehydrate at 120 degrees Fahrenheit for 5 minutes.
6 Serve generously covered with **pad thai sauce**
  {see recipe page 35} and **cashew sour cream**
  {see recipe page 34}. Garnish with slice of lime.

THE MAGAZINE OF NORTHEAST FLORIDA FOR 27 YEARS

JACKSONVILLE

SEPTEMBER 2011

JACKSONVILLEMAG.COM

THE FOOD ISSUE

$3.95 JACKSONVILLEMAG.COM

09>

0 189036 5

PLUS: 28TH ANNUAL CARING CHEFS ★ URGENT CARE ON THE FIRST COAST ★ GET TO KNOW JAGUARS STAR MARCEDES LEWIS ★ DINING HALL OF FAME

69

Our Pad Thai as featured on the cover of *Jacksonville Magazine*

DESSERTS

Ambrosia

yields 1 quart

ingredients

1 pineapple
2 cups **vanilla crème**
{see recipe page 37}
1 cup shredded coconut
1 cup raisins
1 Tbsp lemon juice
1/8 tsp salt

directions

1 Peel and core the pineapple, then dice into small pieces.
2 Combine all ingredients in large mixing bowl.

Lemon Date Bar

yields 1- 9"x13" pan

ingredients

crust:
3 cups pecans
¼ cup maple sugar
1/8 tsp cinnamon
1/8 tsp salt

topping:
1 Tbsp lemon zest
½ cup shredded coconut
2 cups walnuts

filling:
20 pitted dates, soaked 20 minutes
2 cups raisins, soaked 20 minutes
1/3 cup lemon juice
2 Tbsp lemon zest
1 Tbsp vanilla extract
¼ tsp salt

directions

1 Pulse all **crust** ingredients in food processor.
2 Press crust into the bottom of a large glass pan.
3 Drain dates and raisins.
4 Pulse all **filling** ingredients in food processor.
5 Layer the filling evenly over the crust in the glass pan.
6 Chop walnuts in food processor.
7 Combine all **topping** ingredients and layer over filling.
8 Refrigerate for 1 hour to set. Serve with **vanilla crème**
{see recipe page 37}

71

Cobbler

yields 1- 8"x8" pan

ingredients

cobbler:
3 red apples
2 green apples
1/3 cup raisins
1 Tbsp maple syrup
1 Tbsp cinnamon
1 tsp vanilla
pinch salt

topping:
1 cup pecans
2 dates, pitted
pinch salt

directions

1 Core apples, then shred with a grater. Squeeze out
excess liquid through a strainer.
2 Combine all **cobbler** ingredients in a large mixing bowl.
3 Press cobbler into pan.
4 Pulse all **topping** ingredients in food processor to a crumbly consistancy.
5 Layer crust over the cobbler. Dehydrate for 1 hour to warm.
6 Serve with **vanilla ice cream**
{see recipe page 72}

Ice Cream

yields 1 quart

ingredients

1 ½ cups cashews, soaked 1- 2 hours
1 cup filtered water
¾ cup agave
½ cup coconut meat
½ Tbsp vanilla
½ tsp lemon juice
pinch salt

directions

1 Drain and rinse cashews well.
2 In Vitamix, blend all ingredients until smooth and creamy.
3 Pour into ice cream maker and follow manufacturers instructions.
4 Freeze immediately.

Cinnamon Rolls

yields 15 rolls

ingredients

dough:
6 cups almond pulp
   {see recipe page 82}
1 cup ground flax
1 Tbsp cinnamon
3 Tbsp agave
pinch salt

filling:
6 cups pitted dates
6 Tbsp maple syrup
3 Tbsp vanilla extract
3 Tbsp lemon juice
1 Tbsp cinnamon

directions

1 Homogenize all **dough** ingredients in food processor until smooth.
   Set aside.
2 Homogenize all **filling** ingredients in food processor until smooth.
3 Add 1/3 of the **filling** to the **dough** and mix well.
4 Evenly spread the dough out onto a teflex and mesh
   lined dehydrator tray. You may need to use some flour.
5 Spread the filling evenly over the dough with a spatula.
6 • OPTIONAL   • Sprinkle **candied pecans** over the filling
{see recipe page 79}   {see recipe page 79}
7 Roll into a large tube shape.
8 Dehydrate for 2 1/2 hours at 125 degrees Fahrenheit.
9 Slice into 15 even pieces to serve.

Blueberry Parfait

serves 4

ingredients

1 cup **vanilla crème**
   {see recipe page 37}
2 cups fresh or frozen blueberries
½ cup **candied pecans**
   {see recipe page 79}

directions

1 Line four martini glasses with an inch of **vanilla crème.**
2 Evenly disperse blueberries in each glass.
3 Layer on the remaining **vanilla crème**.
4 Sprinkle **candied pecans** over each glass.

agave

To produce agave nectar from the Agave tequiliana plant, juice is expressed from the core of the agave. Raw agave nectar is sweeter than honey, and has a much lower glycemic load than table sugar.

cacao

Essential fatty acids found in cacao help the body raise good cholesterol and lower bad cholesterol. The high levels of antioxidants in cacao reduce free radicals in the body.

73

flours

When grinding nuts or seeds into flour, make sure your blender is bone dry.

maca

Maca is a potent herb that has been found effective in increasing energy levels and stimulating metabolic functions, as well as relieving pain, fighting carcinogens, and even increasing libido!

Chocolate Torte

yields 1 pie

ingredients

filling:
1 cup almond butter
1 cup filtered water
½ cup cacao powder
¼ cup agave
2 Tbsp **date paste**
  {see recipe page 32}
1 ½ Tbsp coconut oil
1 Tbsp tamari
½ Tbsp vanilla extract

crust:
1 ½ cups pecans
2 Tbsp maple sugar
½ Tbsp cinnamon
pinch salt

directions

1 Pulse all **crust** ingredients in food processor into small crumbs.
2 Press crust into the bottom of a pie pan.
3 In Vitamix, blend all **filling** ingredients until smooth.
4 Pour filling evenly over crust.
5 • OPTIONAL • Decorate the pie with a swirled marble pattern of **vanilla crème** {see recipe page 37}
6 Freeze torte until it sets, or becomes hard.

Brownies

yields 1dz brownies

ingredients

3 ½ cups cashews
2 ¼ cups cacao powder
 1 pinch salt
¾ cup maple syrup
1/3 cups agave
½ Tbsp vanilla extract

directions

1 Grind cashews, cacao powder, and salt into a fine flour in the food processor. Place in large mixing bowl.
2 In another mixing bowl whisk all remaining ingredients into a thick syrup.
3 Add syrup to the cashew mixture and mix well.
4 Use a small ice cream scoop to form brownie balls.
5 Refrigerate and serve with **vanilla ice cream** {see recipe page 72}

75

Ganache Pie

yields 1 pie

ingredients

filling:
1 ½ cups cashews
1 cup cacao powder
¾ cup water
½ cup agave
½ cup coconut oil
2 Tbsp maple syrup
½ Tbsp vanilla extract
pinch salt

crust:
1 ½ cups pecans
2 Tbsp maple sugar
½ Tbsp cinnamon
pinch salt

directions

1 Combine all **crust** ingredients in food processor into fine crumbs.
2 Press crust into the bottom of a pie pan.
3 In Vitamix, blend all **filling** ingredients until smooth.
4 Pour filling evenly over crust and refrigerate.

Strawberry Lemon Cheesecake

yields 1 - 8" pie

crust:
1 cup macadamia nuts
3 pitted dates

filling:
1 ¼ cups cashews,
    soaked 1- 2 hours
½ lb frozen strawberries
½ cup coconut oil
¼ cup agave
¼ cup lemon juice
¼ cup filtered water
½ Tbsp vanilla extract

directions

1 Drain and rinse cashews well.
2 Combine all **crust** ingredients in food processor into small crumbs.
3 Press crust into the bottom of a small pie pan.
4 In Vitamix, blend all **filling** ingredients until smooth.
5 Pour filling evenly over crust and refrigerate.

Pumpkin Pie

yields 1 - 8" pie

ingredients

crust:
2 cups pecans
2 Tbsp maple sugar
2 Tbsp raisins
pinch of salt

filling:
¾ cups cashews,
    soaked 1- 2 hours
¾ cup carrot juice
¾ cup coconut oil
1/3 cup agave
1/3 cup maple syrup
2 Tbsp pumpkin pie spice
½ Tbsp vanilla extract
pinch salt

directions

1 Drain and rinse cashews well.
2 Combine all **crust** ingredients in food processor into small crumbs.
3 Press crust into the bottom of a small pie pan.
4 In Vitamix, blend all **filling** ingredients until smooth.
5 Pour filling evenly over crust and refrigerate.

Key Lime Pie

yields 1 - 8" pie

ingredients

crust:
1 cup macadamia nuts
1 cup cashews
¼ cup shredded coconut
2 Tbsp agave
1 tsp vanilla extract
pinch of salt

filling:
1 cup cashews,
    soaked 1- 2 hours
¾ cup coconut meat
¾ cup key lime juice
½ cup agave
½ cup coconut oil
2 Tbsp vanilla extract
pinch of salt

directions

1 Drain and rinse **filling** cashews well.
2 Combine all **crust** ingredients in food processor into small crumbs.
3 Press crust into the bottom of a small pie pan.
4 In Vitamix, blend all **filling** ingredients until smooth.
5 Pour filling evenly over crust and refrigerate.

Apple cobbler

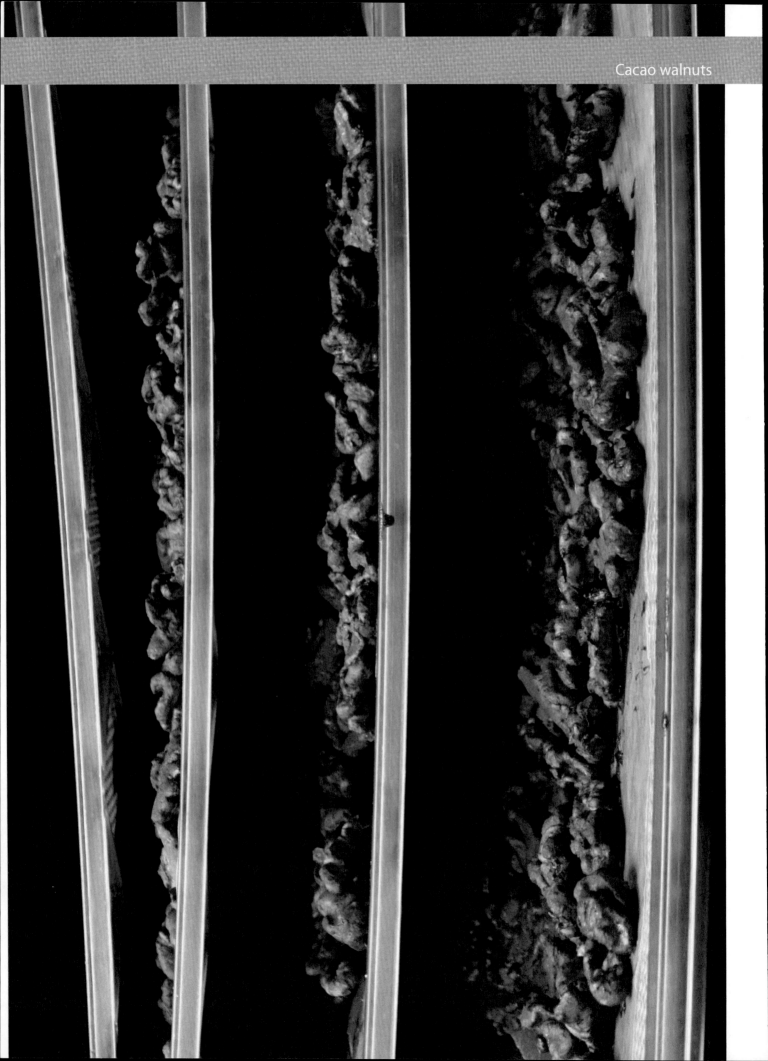

Candied Pecans

yields 1 quart

ingredients

4 cups pecans, soaked 10- 12 hours
1/3 cup agave
1/3 cup maple syrup
¼ cup maple sugar
½ Tbsp orange zest
½ Tbsp cinnamon
2 tsp olive oil
2 tsp orange juice
1 tsp salt

directions

1 Soak pecans 10 to 12 hours. Drain and rinse well.
2 Combine all ingredients in a large mixing bowl.
3 Spread about 4 cups of pecans at a time onto teflex and mesh lined dehydrator trays.
4 Place in dehydrator for 14 hours at 120°Fahrenheil.
5 Flip pecans off teflex sheets and dehydrate another 14 hours.
6 Let cool, break apart, then refrigerate or freeze.

Cacao Walnuts

yields 10 cups

ingredients

10 cups walnuts, soaked 10-12 hours
1 cup agave
1 cup cacao powder
¼ cup maple syrup
2 Tbsp olive oil
1 Tbsp salt
1 Tbsp maple sugar
1 tsp cayenne
1 tsp chili powder
½ tsp vanilla extract

directions

1 Drain and rinse walnuts well.
2 Whisk all ingredients except walnuts until smooth.
3 Combine all ingredients in a large mixing bowl.
4 Spread about 4 cups of walnuts at a time onto teflex and mesh lined dehydrator trays.
5 Place in dehydrator overnight at 120°Fahrenheit.
6 Flip walnuts off teflex sheets and dehydrate another 12 hours.
7 Let cool, break apart, then refrigerate in sealed container.

Cookie Dough

yields 10 cookies

ingredients

2 ½ cups dry cashews
1 ¾ cups raw oats
¾ cup maple syrup
¼ cup filtered water
1 Tbsp vanilla extract
1 tsp salt

directions

1 Grind cashews and oats to a fine flour in a very dry food processor and sift twice.
2 Add all other ingredients in a food processor to a dough-like consistency.
3 • **OPTIONAL** • In a large mixing bowl, combine batter with raisins, dried fruit, chocolate, or nuts of your choice.
4 Use a large ice cream scoop to form cookies.
5 Place on teflex and mesh lined dehydrator trays.
6 Dehydrate for 4 hours at 120°Fahrenheit.

Smoothies

each yields 1 glass

STRAWBERRY FIELDS
1 frozen banana
¼ cup frozen strawberry
8 oz coconut water

PURPLE HAZE
1 frozen banana
¼ cup frozen blueberry
8 oz coconut water

ISLAND PARADISE
1 frozen banana
¼ cup pineapple chunks
8 oz coconut water

directions

In Vitamix, blend all ingredients for each recipe.

Juices

each yields 1 glass

ingredients

THE GLEAM
1 inch ginger
1 apple
3 carrots

END OF PARALYSIS
slice of lemon
4 stalks celery
2 leaves kale
½ cucumber

ROOTED IN COURAGE
1 inch ginger
¼ beet
4 carrots

GREEN DREAM MACHINE
1 inch ginger
slice of lemon
2 leaves kale
3 stalks celery
1 green apple

directions

Place all ingredients into a juicer for each recipe.

Almond Milk

yields 1 quart

ingredients

2 cups almonds, soaked 10-12 hours
6 cups filtered water

directions

1 Drain and rinse almonds well.
2 In Vitamix, blend the almonds and water on high for at least 30 seconds.
3 Pour through a nut bag or cheesecloth and gently milk the sack until dry.
4 Save the **almond pulp** for future recipes.
5 {*optional*} Add 1 Tbsp agave and 1 tsp vanilla extract in each drink to serve.

Milkshakes

each yields 1 glass

ingredients

BANANA MILK
1 frozen banana
10 oz **almond milk** {see recipe above}
1 tsp agave
1 drop vanilla extract

STRAWBERRY MILK
¼ cup frozen strawberry
10 oz **almond milk** {see recipe above}
1 tsp agave
1 drop vanilla extract

CHOCOLATE MILK
10 oz **almond milk** {see recipe above}
2 Tbsp cacao powder
1 tsp agave
1 drop vanilla extract

UNIVERSE DRINK
1 frozen banana
4 oz coconut water
4 oz **almond milk** {see recipe above}
1 tbsp agave
2 Tbsp cacao powder
1 tsp goji powder
½ tsp maca powder
1 drop vanilla extract

directions

In Vitamix, blend all ingredients for each recipe.

Coconut Milk

yields 1 glass

ingredients

8 oz coconut water
2 oz coconut meat

directions

In Vitamix, blend coconut water and coconut meat.

Universe drink

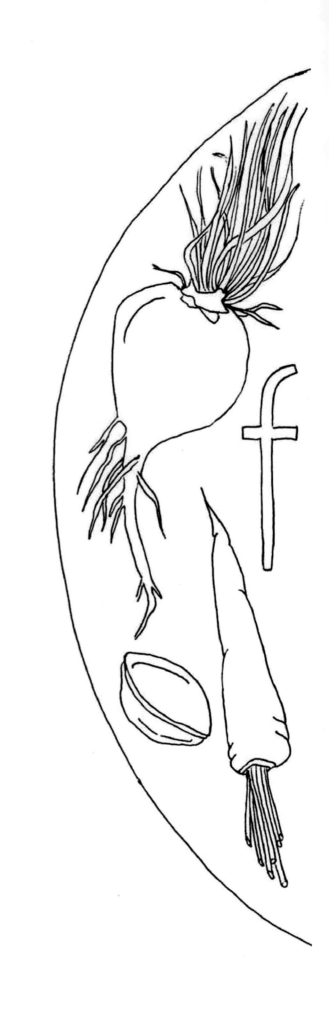

conclusion

More and more, people are awakening to the reality of where our food comes from. Whether one eats animals, vegetables, seeds, or nuts, our earth is the bed from which they are grown.

What we do to the earth we do unto ourselves. I'm reminded every time I fly in an airplane over the land just how much the composition of our bodies looks like the terrain below.

Rivers and canals like veins and arteries and mounds of earth like muscles divided by mineral rich mountains appearing like bones and vertebra.

Roughly seventy percent of the earth is made up of water just as our bodies. Astronauts become aware of the oneness of our planet simply by seeing it from a distance.[1] The raw food diet gave me that distance, affording me a feeling of connectedness to everything around me.

These recipes fueled my journey and gave me vitality.

When asked if I have a favorite recipe, I am reminded of my mother's response when asked to choose her favorite child.

"They are all like fingers of my hand," she said, "though different, loved equally and connected to the whole."

Warm apple cobbler with vanilla ice cream versus chocolate torte topped with drunken banana? Impossible.

I am not 100% raw 100% of the time, nor do I feel one has to be in order to attain health benefits. Personally, I don't refuse food that is handed to me. I gratefully accept it as an offering. I also dine out and enjoy trying new dishes in every country, from every culture.

But I definitely notice that when my percentage of cooked food becomes more than 30% of my diet, I gain weight and lose energy. I do believe food is our medicine and as such we should watch our dosage which is as individual as our doshas. [2]

Whatever your dosage of raw and cooked may be, I hope you will enjoy our recipes, add your own hand (*beetha*) and pass it on.

Much love and gratitude from all of us at The Present Moment Café.

back row, left to right: Natalie, Grayson, Susan, Kelly, Kimberly, Sandy, Yvette, Hugo
second row, left to right: Patty, Angela, Lindsay, Molly Jane, Mike, Dave, Ian, Melissa, Sargon, Victoria, Lora
bottom row, left to right: Casey, Nate, Bosco, Alex, Monica, Clara

[1] As Edgar Mitchell of Apollo 14 said in his autobiography, *The Way of the Explorer*: "What I experienced during that three-day trip home was nothing short of an overwhelming sense of connectedness. I actually felt what is described as 'the ecstasy of unity.'"
[2] A dosha is one of three bodily humors that make up one's constitution according to Ayurveda. The central concept is the theory that health exists when there is a balance between three fundamental doshas called Vata, Pitta and Kapha.

food for thought

Put your hands on the keyboard and follow these issues closely.

There is a real threat to us and the planet that has cropped up...

Genetically Modified Organisms (GMOs).

How is it that man has come to control and mess with seeds?

Seeds were given to us by either Nature, God, or Aliens, whichever your belief may be. Man didn't create them and man doesn't have a right to legislate them. We have a fundamental right to grow and consume any seed whether raw or cooked.

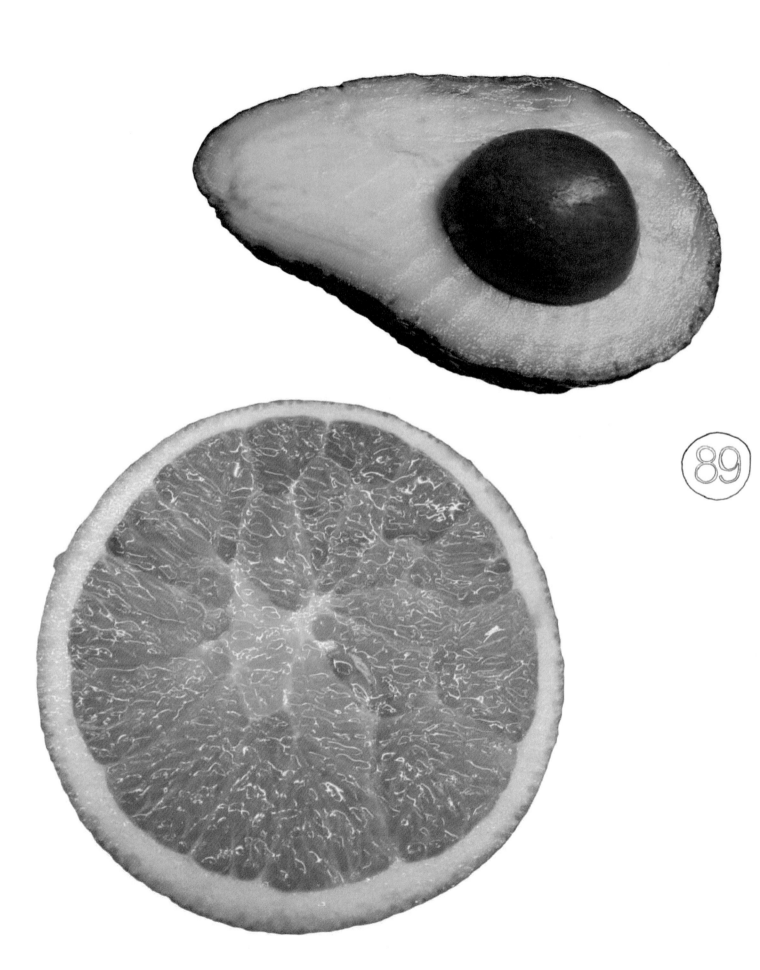

89

customer reviews

ON A TEN POINT SCALE, THIS PLACE IS A 15!
Posted September 17, 2007 at happycow.com

Whether you are into raw foods or not, whether you are even a vegetarian/vegan or not, please give The Present Moment Café a try. You will not be disappointed! The charming quality of the servers and their attentive and prompt service, the quirky, eclectic decor, including some really wonderful artwork, all serve as a backdrop to the amazing and creatively presented food. Everything tastes so good, looks so good and is so good for you, there is no downside here.

I brought my sister (I'm vegan, she's not) and we both enjoyed our meal so much. Our server cheerfully and knowledgeably answered many questions. We had the Portobello mushroom appetizer (so good, we ordered a 2nd one), Chile Relleños, Portobello Croquettes, Kale Salad and fruit tartlet for dessert. We ate a huge amount of food, and still took home enough for lunch the next day. I felt the prices were more than fair, considering the quality and the quantity of the food. Can't wait to go back! Well done to the whole staff for an amazing experience!

WORLD CLASS CUISINE AND, SURPRISE, IT'S VEGAN!
Posted September 29, 2007 at tripadvisor.com

The Present Moment Café is one of St. Augustine's off-the-main treasures. Insiders are devoted to this place. Walk in the door and inhale an addictive herbal fragrance that will seduce your senses. I'm a meat/chicken/fish eater, in moderation, and consider myself a healthful eater, but I was wary of this vegan/raw food theme. I am now a convert. Not only is this food healthy, it is creative, delicious, filling, and sensuous. The restaurant is unpretentious but sophisticated in a laid back way. It's on West King Street, which many of the uninitiated local yokels consider to be the wrong side of town. But the think-outside-the-boxsters (including PMC owner Yvette) are appreciating the potential of this neglected yet up-and-coming neighborhood. The menu is imaginative and delicious. And the organic wine list, while small, is good quality. The daily specials are can't-go-wrong splendid, and the desserts are exquisite (my fave is the cacao torte with a hint of chile spice and rum-marinated banana garnish - omigod).

I thought vegan / veggie food would be like eating sawdust. Present Moment Cafe not only destroys that bias but immerses you in a delightful culinary experience that provides a unique, delicious meal and leaves you feeling like you've done your body a healthy favor! Five stars!

LIFE CHANGING
Posted June 26, 2011 at tripadvisor.com

My first experience with raw food dining was so fantastic I am now adding raw foods to my diet on a daily basis. My friend and I sampled the kale/avocado salad, collard wrap, tacos of life and pesto pasta. They were all fabulous. For dessert the apple pecan cobbler was just as flavorful as any baked version. Everything was beautifully presented, full of distinct flavors and very filling. The server was extremely helpful and knowledgeable about ingredients and preparation. Any raw food novice would find plenty to like here. In fact, it's not really obvious that the food is uncooked. I can't wait to return to the Present Moment.

RUN, DON'T WALK, TO THIS RESTAURANT!

Posted April 21, 2010 at happycow.com

I am from New York and pride myself on having eaten in some of the world's best restaurants.
Present Moment is THE best restaurant, vegetarian or not, that I have ever eaten in. The food
is art. It is beautifully prepared, beautifully presented and absolutely delicious. I have been
vegan/vegetarian for years and had been skeptical about raw food; I never felt well after eating it.
But by the time we got to St. Augustine, I just wanted healthy food and so ended up at Present
Moment. Frankly, I wasn't expecting much. The raw food was amazing and only made me feel
more energized. We ate every single meal there for the rest of our vacation, except one (and we
regretted that). We are awaiting the Present Moment cook book and have begun the transition
to eating all raw. Oh, and one more thing. Yvette, the owner, is a visionary and her staff is
knowledgeable, committed and extremely hard working. The service, too, was beyond anything
I've experienced. Truly, I would go back to St. Augustine just for Present Moment.

It's that good.

RAW DELIGHT

Posted February 1, 2010 at tripadvisor.com

Anthony Bourdain notwithstanding, raw food, properly done, can be every bit as satisfying
as more traditional cuisine, and here, they not only do it properly, they do it expertly. I am
neither a vegan nor a vegetarian, but I am a foodie and while I do like to eat healthy, I am not
a fanatic about it. I've had raw food before, but not like this. The Present Moment has the feel
of a college coffeehouse -- it's small, artsy, unpretentiously bohemian, and the people here
really enjoy what they do. And they do it very, very well. I've found that it doesn't really help to
describe raw food, because it does not quite convey the experience. You really have to try it for
yourself. For example, imagine "vanilla ice cream" that is completely non-dairy and made from
emulsified cashews. Doesn't sound terrific, does it? Trust me, it's delicious. Some people have
a hard time overcoming their prejudices. There are fancier places, more pretentious places,
and more expensive places, but none that give you more bang for your buck than this place.
And it's good for you, too. Check out their website, then do yourself a favor and stop by
next time you're in town. If you have an open mind, you will be surprised and delighted.
We were, and we'll be back

MIND = BLOWN

Posted October 2, 2010 at tripadvisor.com

One of the most spectacular and creative arrangements of raw foods and vegetables that we
have ever had. Almost nothing like this restaurant exists in most metropolitan areas. Some
truly daring and wonderful dishes that are served incredibly beautifully. Having said that, as
we waited for our creative and scrupulously vegan desserts (e.g. ice cream made with cashews,
sea salt, agave and coconut--better than anything Cold Stone Creamery has ever had) Don't
miss this place. You'll never find another like it!!

index

photography credits:

handmade in the present moment

author: yvette schindler, owner of the present moment café
creative director: molly jane hammond, molly jane design

index

index

index

handmade in the present moment
© yvette schindler, 2010
author: yvette schindler, owner of the present moment café
creative director: molly jane hammond, molly jane design

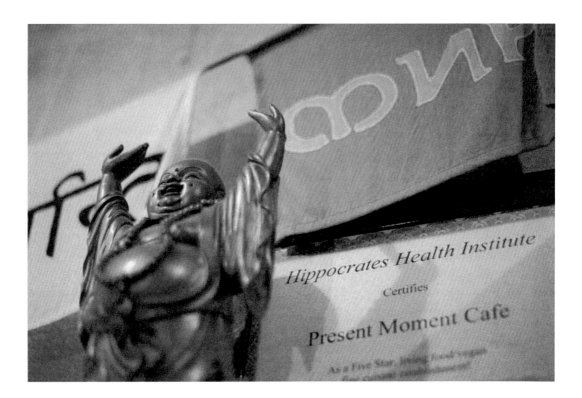

Love&Gratitude

Notes

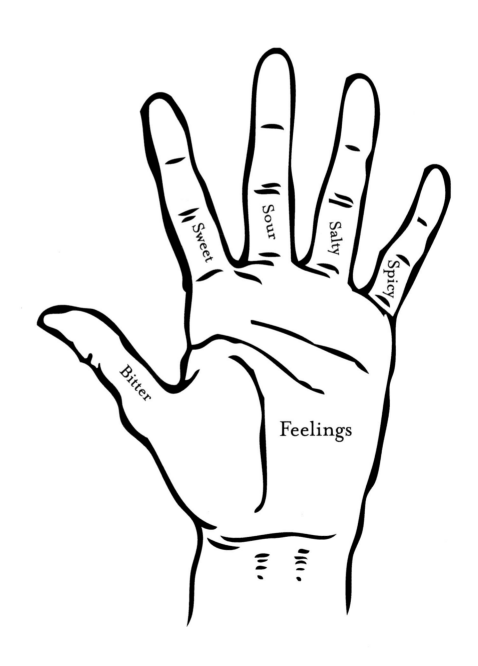

Notes